Gettysburg

The Nature of a Battlefield

Photos and descriptions by **Patricia Rich**

Edited by **Lana Taylor**

GETTYSBURG PUBLISHING

Gettysburg

The Nature of a Battlefield

Gettysburg Publishing LLC

Please go to www.gettysburgpublishing.com
for all our other titles.

Several descriptions within this book contain historic uses for, and folklore about, certain plants and birds. This is for information only, and in no way suggests that the reader should follow suit. Gettysburg Publishing LLC and Patricia Rich, the author, do not recommend or condone the catching, picking, or consumption of any of the species within this volume, and will not be held responsible for such actions.

Library of Congress Control Number: 2015938864
ISBN-978-0-9838631-5-1

Patricia Rich
Photographer/Author

Patricia Rich was raised in southern Maryland, just down the road from the Surratt House and Tavern in Clinton, Maryland. Family trips to the Manassas Battlefield, Dr. Mudd's Historic Site, Point Lookout, and Gettysburg only fueled her avid interest in history. This interest would eventually lead to her marrying a like-minded individual, Ken Rich, and honeymooning in Gettysburg nearly 30 years ago. Pat developed an interest in photography, and encouraged by friends, began posting photos online, and eventually creating the *Gettysburg Landscapes Calendar*, now in its fifth year. Beginning with photos of the surrounding landscape and monuments, she began to take notice of the local flora and fauna, including them in her extensive portfolio. Pat has partnered with **Gettysburg Publishing** for future projects, including photography and graphic design services. She sells her photography and photographic products, including calendars, prints, postcards, note cards and gifts, at **Gettysburg Battlefield Books and Collectibles**, as well as other shops, in Gettysburg.

Lana Taylor
Editor

Lana Taylor is currently a graduating senior at The Pennsylvania State University, pursuing a major degree in Biology and a minor degree in Human Development and Family Studies. For the last four years Lana has served as the Course Assistant to Samuel Richards and the Sociology 119 course. Additionally, she is currently a Research Assistant in The SHAARP lab (The Study of Healthy Aging and Applied Research Programs). Lana is also the Marketing Director to The Multicultural Women's Forum, an organization dedicated to the empowerment of women in professional settings. Her future goal is to become a licensed Occupational Therapist. In the Fall of 2015 she will begin her graduate studies in Occupational Therapy at The University of Illinois –Chicago. Originally from Chicago, Lana looks forward to a career dedicated to providing therapy services to the most underserved areas of the city.

There are so many people to recognize for their contribution to this book that it is difficult to know where to start.

First, and foremost, there is my husband, Ken Rich, whose patience during this entire process, both on and off the battlefield, was boundless.

Thanks to my many battlefield friends, especially those who encouraged me to continue with my photography and were early supporters of my work in this endeavor.

I would also like to recognize the many park rangers and licensed battlefield guides of the Gettysburg National Military Park for their understanding each time I wandered off a little ways or lagged behind on a tour to get a picture of this and that, much of which is contained in this guide.

No small measure of gratitude goes to my editor, Lana Taylor, who came into this project toward the end, and eagerly tackled the task of verifying my identifications and descriptions. And, thanks also to Randy Drais and his niece, Alicia Drais-Parrillo, who hooked me up with Lana.

I would also like to recognize my friends at Gettysburg Publishing, Kevin Drake, Bernadette Atkins, and Lisa Shower, who encouraged me to take on this project, giving me free rein with its content and design, and allowing me the time to do it properly.

There Will Come Soft Rains

by Sara Teasdale

There will come soft rains and the smell of the ground,
And swallows circling with their shimmering sound;

And frogs in the pools, singing at night,
And wild plum trees in tremulous white,

Robins will wear their feathery fire,
Whistling their whims on a low fence-wire;

And not one will know of the war, not one
Will care at last when it is done.

Not one would mind, neither bird nor tree,
If mankind perished utterly;

And Spring herself, when she woke at dawn,
Would scarcely know that we were gone.

Flowers – Yellow

Thin-leaved Sunflower *(Helianthus decapetalus)*

Normally found in areas with a moderate water supply, this sturdy perennial can make a dramatic statement in any landscape. The flower heads attract a variety of insects, and the seeds serve as food for gamebirds and songbirds, as well as small animals such as deer, rabbits and groundhogs.

Rough-stemmed Goldenrod *(Solidago rugosa)*

Found mainly in open fields, roadsides and edges of woods, it forms large masses in areas that were once cultivated. While this showy plant is often blamed for causing hay fever, that condition is actually caused by ragweed.

Black-eyed Susan *{Rudbeckia hirta}*

Grows in fields, prairies and open woods. This biennial forms a rosette of leaves the first year, followed by flowers the second year. The roots can be used (in a warm infusion) as an astringent or wash for sores and swellings. The Ojibwa used it as a poultice for snake bites.

Trout Lily *{Erythronium americanum}*

One of the most common spring wildflowers, it is found in sizable colonies in rich woods and meadows. The name refers to the similarity between the leaf markings and those of brown and brook trout.

Rough-fruited Cinquefoil *{Potentilla recta}*

Located on roadsides, in dry fields and waste places. It is seldom eaten by livestock and is considered one of the most rapidly increasing weeds. The plant may reproduce by seed or vegetatively by sprouting new shoots.

Butter-and-eggs/Common Toadflax *(Linaria vulgaris)*

Considered a noxious weed in most areas, this plant can be found in dry fields, waste places, and roadsides. An orange path on the lower lip leads to nectar and serves as a "honey guide" for insects. The common name refers to the color combination of the corolla.

Common Buttercup *{Ranunculus acris}*

Located in old fields, meadows and disturbed areas, this is one of the tallest and most common buttercups. Somewhat poisonous, the sap from its stems and leaves is acrid, discouraging animals from grazing upon it.

Birdsfoot Trefoil *(Lotus corniculatus)*

Introduced from Europe, this plant can be found in fields and on roadsides. The shape of the flower resembles a bird's foot, hence the common name. It is used in agriculture as a forage plant and may be used as an alternative to alfalfa in poor soils.

Golden Ragwort *(Packera aurea)*

Found in wet meadows, swamps and moist woods, this perennial is also known as Squaw Weed and Life Root. This plant was an important treatment among Native Americans for reproductive conditions. The foliage is shunned by most herbivores due to its toxicity, but sheep are more tolerant and will eat it.

Yellow Wood Sorrel *(Oxalis stricta)*

This plant is native to North America and grows in woodlands, meadows and disturbed areas, both as a perennial and an annual. All parts of the plant are edible with a distinct tangy flavor; the leaves can be used to make a drink similar in flavor to lemonade. It contains large amounts of vitamin C.

Evening Primrose *(Oenothera biennis)*

Growing in fields and roadsides, the flowers of this night-blooming biennial open in the evening and close by noon or earlier. The blooms can open in as little as 15 minutes. The first-year roots are edible and the seeds are an important bird feed.

Common Mullein *{Verbascum thapsus}*

This biennial, found in fields and on roadsides, has been used for many purposes. Soldiers dipped the flower spikes in grease for use as torches. Tea made from the leaves was used to treat colds, and the flowers and roots were used to treat ailments from earaches to croup.

Prickly Pear *{Opuntia humifusa}*

Found in sandy areas and open, rocky sites, this native plant is the only cactus widespread in the eastern United States. The bristles at the base of the spines are lined with backward-pointing hooks, making them difficult to remove. Its many uses include food, alcohol spirits, dye production and folk medicine.

Common St. John's Wort *(Hypericum perforatum)*

This herb grows in fields, roadsides and waste places. It can cause photodermatitis in animals that graze on it, and is poisonous in large doses. It is known as an herbal treatment for depression, but there can be adverse effects (including light sensitivity) and drug interactions associated with its use.

Japanese Honeysuckle *(Lonicera japonica)*

Located in thickets, roadsides and woodlands, this wood vine introduced from Asia, has escaped from cultivation. It is a threat to native flora and can engulf and choke out trees very quickly. Its sweet nectar is highly attractive to bees and other insects.

Tickseed Sunflower *(Bidens aristosa)*

These flowers are generally found in wet meadows, roadside ditches, abandoned fields and low ground. The prickly fruit of this species is known as beggars' ticks, the little stickers that cling to one's clothing during autumn walks.

Yellow Pond Lily/Bullhead Lily *(Nuphar variegata)*

Located in pondsides and quiet streams, this is the most familiar yellow pond lily in the Northeast. The leaves, stems and flower stalks die back each year and contribute to the organic buildup in lakes and marshes.

Yellow Water Lily *(Nymphaea Mexicana)*

Found in the quiet water of ditches and ponds, the flowers are open from midday to late afternoon. The leaves are generally underwater, unless overcrowded. The plant was first discovered in Mexico, hence its species name.

Giant Sunflower *(Helianthus giganteus)*

This perennial is native to the eastern United States, and is most commonly found in valleys with wet meadows or swamps. The bright, showy seed heads attract birds. However, the stems and leaves can cause skin irritation in humans, and the plant can be fatal to animals if ingested.

Partridge Pea *(Chamaecrista fasciculata)*

A species of legume native to most of the eastern United States, this plant is pollinated only by bees. It will quickly cover disturbed areas, preventing erosion, while allowing other plants to become established. The seed is one of the major food items of northern bobwhite and quail.

Flowers – Orange

Spotted Touch-Me-Not/Jewelweed *(Impatiens capensis)*

Can be found in shaded wetlands and woods. It is especially adapted to hummingbird activity, but is also pollinated by bees and butterflies. The sap of the stems and leaves is said to relieve itching from poison ivy and nettles and is scientifically proven to have fungicidal properties.

Pale Touch-Me-Not/Jewelweed *(Impatiens pallida)*

This soft-stemmed annual, found in wet woods and meadows, is less common than the Spotted Touch-Me-Not. The common name is derived from the triggering of seeds, by touch, from its sensitive, ripe flower. There is also a purple version called the Policeman's Hat.

Kalm's St. John's Wort *(Hypericum kalmianum)*

Located in rocky or sandy soil, this is one of several shrubby St. John's worts. Peter Kalm discovered the plant in America around 1750, so the plant is named in his honor. The common name derives from the fact that the flowers were said to bloom on St. John's Eve, but more often in July or August.

Butterfly Weed/Orange Milkweed *(Asclepias tuberosa)*

Usually found in open dry soil, on roadsides and in fields, this showy plant is often planted in home gardens. Its brilliant flowers attract butterflies, hence its common name. Native Americans would chew its tough roots to treat pleurisy and other pulmonary ailments.

Day Lily *(Hemerocallis fulva)*

Located on roadsides, in meadows and woodland borders. This native of Eurasia was introduced to gardens and has escaped cultivation. It reproduced vegetatively rather than by setting seed. Every part of the plant is mild and edible. The flower pods taste like green beans when cooked.

Blackberry Lily *(Belamcanda chinensis)*

Found on roadsides and in open woods, this Chinese introduction has escaped cultivation. The blackberry-like seed cluster is the origin of its common name. The dried rhizome has long been used in East Asia to treat throat troubles, asthma, swollen liver and spleen, gonorrhea, malaria, and arrow poisoning.

Scarlet Pimpernel *(Anagallis arvensis)*

This attractive annual shows up in sandy soil, waste places and on roadsides. It is sometimes called Poor Man's Weatherglass because it closes its flowers in cloudy or bad weather. The leaves may cause a severe dermatitis, but it was at one time used in a treatment for melancholy.

Flowers – Red/Pink

Cardinal Flower *(Lobelia cardinalis)*

Usually found in damp sites, especially along streams. This species is pollinated chiefly by hummingbirds, since most insects find it difficult to access the long, tubular flowers. The common name may allude to the red robes worn by Roman Catholic cardinals or to the red bird of the same name.

Common Poppy *(Papaver rhoeas)*

Poppies thrive on disturbed ground and tolerate high amounts of lime. The young leaves are cooked like spinach, or used raw as flavoring in soups and salads. The petals make a red syrup used in soups or for coloring. The seeds can be used in cakes, bread, rolls, or pressed for their oil.

Staghorn Sumac *(Rhus typhina)*

This plant, native to eastern North America, can grow under a wide array of conditions, but is most often found in dry and poor soil on which other plants cannot survive. The fruit of sumacs can be collected, soaked and washed in cold water, strained, sweetened and made into a pink lemonade.

Common Cattail *(Typha Latifolia)*

Found in freshwater marshes, ditches and on shorelines, this perennial forms dense stands providing a favorable habitat for red-winged blackbirds and other marsh birds. Native Americans and early colonists used it for food, as most of the plant is edible.

Swamp Milkweed *(Asclepias incarnata)*

Located in swamps, shorelines and thickets, this perennial is a Monarch butterfly host plant. Named in honor of Asklepios, the Greek god of medicine, some species have been used to treat a variety of ailments. The sap of this milkweed is less milky than that of other species.

Common Milkweed *(Asclepias syriaca)*

Found in old fields and roadsides. The plant contains cardiac glycosides, when absorbed by Monarch butterfly larvae, make the larvae and adult butterflies toxic to birds and other predators. These same glycosides, allied to those in Foxglove, are used in treating some heart diseases.

Virginia Rose *(Rosa virginiana)*

Located in clearings, thickets, meadows, clearings, shores, and roadsides. Their fruit, the so-called rose hips which are red and look a lot like a large berry, is rich in vitamin C and can be eaten, made into jam, or steeped to make rose hip tea. The hips can stay on the plant into the winter.

Wild Mint *(Mentha arvensis)*

This native mint can be found mainly in damp to wet places. Wild Mint is an aromatic perennial that has glands containing essential oils. The leaves are used as flavoring in sauces, jellies and beverages. Despite its numerous uses, it is a highly invasive plant.

Bleeding Heart *(Dicentra spectabilis)*

Grows best in moist, dark woodlands. This attractive plant, often found in domestic gardens, is deer resistant. Despite its beauty, isoquinolin-like alkaloids in the plant can cause skin irritations in some people.

Deptford Pink *(Dianthus armeria)*

Located in dry fields and on roadsides, This European introduction, closely related to Carnation, also resembles the Maiden Pink. The common name refers to Deptford, England (now part of London), where the flower was once abundant.

Showy Tick-trefoil *(Desmodium canadense)*

Found in moist open woods and edges of fields. The distinctively jointed fruits break into segments that stick to clothes and animal fur, helping the plant to propegate.

Climbing Boneset/Climbing Hempvine *(Mikania scandens)*

This vine, which has vanilla-scented flowers, can be found in swampy woods, damp ditches, pond margins, and wet creeksides throughout most of the eastern United States. Native Americans used this plant to stop itching. Its clumping vines can force out more desirable species.

New England Aster *(Symphyotrichum novae-angliae)*

It is native to almost every area in North America east of the Rocky Mountains, and grows in wet meadows, thickets, low fields, and moist ground along streams. it provides an important source of late season nectar for bees and Monarch butterflies.

Flowers – Purple/Blue

Crown Vetch *(Coronilla varia)*

This European introduction is often planted along roadsides as a stabilizing perennial, but can also be found in waste places and fields. It is now naturalized in many areas, making a striking groundcover. Like all members of the pea family, vetch adds nitrogen to the soil.

Purple Coneflower *(Echinacea purpurea)*

Usually found in dry open woods and prairies, the genus name is from the Greek echino ("hedgehog"), an allusion to the spiny, brownish central disk. The flowers are used to make an extremely popular herbed tea, purported to help strengthen the immune system.

Spring Beauty *(Claytonia virginica)*

Located in moist woods, thickets and clearings, this perennial is particularly attractive in large patches. It is one of the first plants to bloom in the spring. The tubers have a sweet, chestnut-like flavor and were used by Native Americans and colonists for food.

Garden Phlox *(Phlox paniculata)*

Found in open woods and thickets. Most cultivars are fragrant and thus very attractive to butterflies and hummingbirds. They bear flowers in a variety of colors. This plant has been widely used as a medicinal herb; the leaf extract is used as a laxative and for treating boils.

Dame's Rocket *(Hesperis matronalis)*

Found on roadsides, in open woods, woodlands borders and thickets. An old-fashioned European garden plant, it is now widely naturalized in North America. The fragrance of the flowers is most pronounced at the close of day. Similar in appearance to Garden Phlox, but with a different petal count.

Wild Blue Phlox/Wild Sweet William *(Phlox divaricata)*

Found in rich fields and woods, the mature plants of the eastern version are notched, while the western ones are not. The fragrant flowers, which vary in color (including pink, white, purple and blue) attract butterflies and moths. The roots provide food to rabbits and voles.

Red Clover *(Trifolium pratense)*

Found in mostly wet and dry grasslands, it can also be found in old fields, lawns and roadsides. Clover is planted here as a hay and pasture crop. It stores nitrogen in its root nodules and is used in crop rotation to improve soil fertility.

Bull Thistle *(Cirsium vulgare)* First Year

Found on roadsides, in pastures and waste places, is the spiniest thistle and should be handled only with gloves. It is a biennial, producing a rosette of leaves the first year and an upright flowering stalk the second year. It is a favorite of finches as a food source.

Musk Thistle *(Carduus nutans)*

Located in waste places and fields, meadows and grasslands, but not in excessively wet, dry, or shady conditions. Introduced in the early 19th century, it is considered a noxious weed in several states, since it requires considerable effort to eradicate and cattle may refuse to graze where it grows.

Canadian Thistle *(Cirsium arvense)*

Growing in pastures and roadsides, this European introduction came to the United States by way of Canada, hence its common name. It is a pervasive weed and classified as noxious in most states.

Foxglove *(Digitalis purpurea)*

All parts of this plant are poisonous to humans and some animals, and can be fatal if eaten. However, a compound extracted from the leaves, is used as a medication for heart failure. Foxglove blooms in midsummer in a range of habitats, including open woods and woodland clearings.

Round-lobed Hepatica *(Hepatica nobilis)*

Found in deeply shaded woodland and full-sun grasslands, this member of the buttercup family, is native to eastern North America. Although poisonous in large doses, the leaves and flowers have some medicinal value. Butterflies, moths, bees, flies and beetles are known pollinators.

Ground Ivy *(Glechoma hederacea)*

This common plant has numerous medicinal uses, and is used as a salad green in many countries. It is found in grasslands and wooded areas or wasteland. The fresh herb can be rinsed and steeped in hot water to create an herbal tea which is rich in vitamin C.

Purple Loosestrife *(Lythrum salicaria)*

Found in ditches, wet meadows, and marshes, it has also been introduced in many areas of North America by bee keepers. Due to its abundance of flowers, it provides a large source of nectar for long-tongued insects. It has been used as an astringent medicinal herb to treat diarrhea and dysentery.

Slender Bush Clover *(Lespedeza virginica)*

This plant, a member of the pea family, has escaped cultivation and now occurs wild in dry open woods, thickets and clearings. The plants and seeds are eaten by a variety of livestock and wildlife.

Late Purple Aster *(Symphyotrichum patens)*

A drought-tolerant perennial, it is generally found in dry open woods and dry fields,. The attractive flower blooms from August to October. Over time, multiple stems emerge and the plants become quite bushy and showy. They are beneficial to native bee and butterfly populations.

Chicory (*Cichorium intybus*)

Found in fields, roadsides, and waste places. Only a few flower heads open at a time. While considered a weed by some, it is often sought for its food uses. The roots can be roasted and ground as a coffee substitute or additive, and the leaves used in salad. It is also grown as a forage crop for livestock.

Teasel *(Dipsacus fullonum)*

Growing in old fields and roadsides, this plant was introduced from Europe. The progression of flowers is unique, starting at a center belt and forming two bands. The genus, from the Greek dipsa (thirst), refers to water that accumulates in the cup-like base. The seeds are an important winter food source for birds.

Spiderwort *(Tradescantia virginiana)*

Grows in woodland borders, thickets, meadows and roadsides. This plant is so-named for the leaf arrangement suggesting a squatting spider. Flowers open only in the morning. The hairs found on the stamens are often a subject for microscopic examination because the flowing cytoplasm can be seen easily.

Monkeyflower *(Mimulus ringens)*

Located in wet meadows and along streambanks, the flower resembles a monkey's face, hence its common name. The Mimulus species concentrates sodium chloride and other salts absorbed from the soil and was used by Native Americans and early travelers as a salt substitute to flavor wild game.

Bluets *(Houstonia caerulea)*

Inhabits grassy slopes and fields, thickets and lawns in acidic soil. It often forms striking patches of light blue. Bluets are a native species, but are challenging to get established. They need lean soil and freedom from competition, but will thrive once they find their ideal location.

Common Blue Violet *(Viola sororia)*

Grows in damp woods, moist meadows, lawns and roadsides. Violet leaves are high in vitamins A and C and can be used in salads or cooked as greens. The flowers can be candied and eaten also.

Blue Flag *(Iris versicolor)*

Found in swamps, marshes and wet shorelines, this is a showy native iris of northeastern wetlands. The rhizome is poisonous, but it was dried and used in small amounts as a cathartic and a diuretic by Native Americans and colonists.

Harebell/Bluebell *(Campanula rotundifolia)*

Found on rocky banks and slopes, meadows and shorelines, habitat can contribute to variations in characteristics of this perennial. The genus name means little bell. The common name may allude to its association with witches, who were believed to transform themselves into hares.

Viper's Bugloss *(Echium vulgare)*

Grows in fields, roadsides and waste places, often in limestone soil. An attractive wildflower, this plant is a European species introduced as early as 1683, and considered by many as a weed. Its stiff hairs can penetrate the skin.

Bittersweet Nightshade *(Solanum dulcamara)*

Found in thickets and clearings, this vine is quite distinctive. The leaves and fruit contain the poisonous alkaloid solanine. Its toxin is not fatal, but the berries are attractive to children and can cause poisoning if eaten in a large quantity. Long ago the plant was used in England to counteract witchcraft.

True Forget-me-not *(Myosotis scorpioides)*

Found in streamsides and wet places, it was introduced from Europe and is now naturalized around lakes, ponds and streams. In bud, the tightly coiled flower cluster resembles the tail of a scorpion. It was introduced to the New England area from Europe and was extremely cultivated for ornamental use.

Great Lobelia *(Lobelia siphilitica)*

Inhabits rich lowland woods, meadows and swamps. This blue counterpart to the Cardinal Flower is most desirable for wildflower gardens. The species name is based on the fact that it was a supposed cure for syphilis. The roots contain alkoloids which can cause vomiting.

Columbine *(Aquilegia vulgaris)*

The genus name is derived from the Latin word for eagle as the flower petals resemble an eagle's claw. Found in meadows and woodlands, they are used as food plants by some butterfly and moth caterpillars. The plants and seeds are highly poisonous and can cause severe gastroenteritis and heart palpitations.

Blue Vervain *(Verbena hastata)*

Can be located in damp thickets, shorelines and roadslides. Bumblebees are among its important pollinators. In ancient times some verbenas were thought to be cure-alls among medicinal plants.

Blue-Eyed Grass *(Sisyrinchium angustifolium)*

Blue-eyed grasses, native to meadows and open woodland, belong to the iris family. Their low, clumping, grass-like mounds provide good cover for small wildlife, and they are deer-resistant. An important food source for pollinators (insects and birds), they grow well in hot, humid weather.

Flowers – White

Horse Nettle *(Solanum carolinense)*

This deep-rooted perennial, considered a weed by some, grows in fields, waste places, and cultivated sites. Deep hoeing is required to get rid of horse nettle as it has a deep, hardy root system. Seeds are spread by grazing cattle, but the plant is generally avoided by them.

Queen Anne's Lace *(Dancus carota)*

Often found in dry fields, this plant is an ancestor of the garden carrot and its leaves, when crushed, emit a carrot-like odor. Its long, first-year taproot can be cooked and eaten.

Mayapple; Mandrake *(Podophyllum peltatum)*

Can be found in rich woods and damp shady clearings. The leaves, roots and seeds are poisonous if ingested in large quantities; however, in small quantities, the roots were used by Native Americans as a cathartic. When ripe, the fruit is edible and can be used in jellies, for juice or eaten fresh.

Multiflora Rose *(Rosa multiflora)*

This invasive species, found in fields, roadsides and wooded areas, is sold as a living hedge by some nurseries. On a positive note, while considered by some as a noxious weed, it can provide excellent wildlife cover.

Moth Mullein *(Verbascum blattaria)*

Old fields and roadsides are the habitat of this attractive plant. Moth mullein has long been known as an effective cockroach repellent. Seeds buried dormant in 1879 were dug up, planted in favorable conditions and yielded a 50% germination rate, an incredible 120 years later.

Ox-eye Daisy *(Leucanthemum vulgare)*

Often found in meadows, pastures and roadsides. An extremely common, weed-like species, Ox-eye Daisies are disliked by farmers because they can produce an unwanted flavor in milk if eaten by cattle.

Turtlehead *(Chelone glabra)*

A herbaceous plant found in wetlands and on forest riverbanks, it is deer resistant. Butterflies, hummingbirds, bumblebees and other beneficial insects visit to drink the nectar. Turtlehead provides cover for frogs and toad, and is a host plant for the Baltimore checkerspot butterfly.

Watercress *(Nasturtium officinale)*

A member of the mustard family, in its native habitat, watercress easily naturalizes in springs, streams and even boggy ground. Fortified with more than 15 essential vitamins and minerals, even since ancient times its health giving properties have been highly valued. This is a very invasive species.

Black Elderberry *(Sambucus nigra)*

For people wishing to support native butterfly and bird species, native elderberry species are a good choice for planting. While uncooked berries and other parts of the plants are poisonous to humans, the ripe, cooked berries (pulp and skin) are edible, and used for jams, pies and beverages.

Rue Anemone *(Thalictrum thalictroides)*

A member of the buttercup family, it is native to woodlands in eastern North America. Found in dry deciduous woodlands, on wooded slopes, and thinly wooded bluffs, it offers only pollen to insect visitors. Because its foliage is toxic, it is largely ignored by mammals.

Virgin's Bower *(Clematis virginiana)*

A native vine most often found in moister settings, such as along stream banks or in floodplains, its showy flowers attract butterflies and hummingbirds. The plant is toxic, but the Cherokee included an infusion (with milkweed) for treating backache and an infusion from the roots for kidney ailments.

Common Blackberry *(Rubus allegheniensis)*

Its habitats include woodlands, thickets, fence rows, roadsides and railbeds, and abandoned pastures. Bees, long-tongued and short-tongued, are attracted to this plant, as are other insects. A variety of birds and animals feed on the fruit, stems, or foliage; humans also enjoy the fruit.

Eastern Daisy Fleabane *(Erigeron annuus)*

Native to North America, this plant is found in 43 of the lower 48 states. It often colonizes disturbed areas such as pastures, abandoned fields, roadsides, railways, and waste areas. Flowers are pollinated by a variety of bees, as well as flies. Some mammals eat the foliage, flowers. and stems.

Foxglove Beardtongue *(Penstemon digitalis)*

Blooming from May to July, beardtongue prefers fields, prairies and open woods, and attracts a variety of moths, butterflies, and hummingbirds. Some Native Americans used the plants to treat chills, fever, and toothache pain.

Yarrow *(Achillea millefolium)*

Yarrow attracts ladybirds, hoverflies, and predatory wasps, which drink the nectar and then use insect pests as food for their larvae. Several cavity-nesting birds, including the common starling, use yarrow to line their nests. Its essential oil kills the larvae of the tiger mosquito.

Venice Mallow *(Hibiscus trionum)*

Blooming from July through August, it prefers disturbed sites, waste ground, cultivated fields, pastures, and roadsides. A difficult weed to control, its seeds can remain dormant underground for several decades. It has attractive flowers that open for only a short period during the day.

White Vervain *(Verbena urticifolia)*

A herbaceous plant in the vervain family, it can be weedy or invasive. White vervain is native to North America, except in the western states. Found in fields, roadsides, forest borders, open rights-of-way, and forest riverbanks, this plant is attractive to bees, butterflies and birds.

White Avens *(Geum canadense)*

Located at woodland edges and openings, thickets, and in open woodlands, these flowers attract various insects, including bees, wasps, flies, and beetles. The foliage is not attractive to white-tailed deer.

Flowering Spurge *(Euphorbia corollata)*

Native to North America, flowering spurge is an open land species, preferring drier soils. It is commonly found in grasslands, on roadsides, old fields, and in woodlands. The sap of many spurge family plants is caustic or a skin and eye irritant, although it has traditional medicinal uses.

Bloodroot *(Sanguinaria canadensis)*

Native to North America, these perennial plants can be found growing in moist to dry woods and thickets and along streams. Bloodroot produces a red natural dye used by Native American artists. It was also used as a curative, but recent studies indicate that it may be more detrimental than helpful.

Dutchman's Breeches *(Dicentra cucullaria)*

A native perennial found in rich woodland soil, their name comes from the shape of their flowers. Native Americans and early colonials considered the plant useful in treating syphillis, skin conditions and blood purification. However, it can cause dermatitis in some people.

Cutleaf Toothwort *(Dentaria laciniata syn. Cardamine concatenata)*

Cutleaf toothwort, a member of the mustard family, is a perennial, woodland wildflower native to eastern North America. It does well in rocky areas and is often accompanied by Spring Beauty and Dutchman's Breeches. The tubers of this plant were once a minor food source for the Passenger Pigeon (extinct).

Pokeweed *(Phytolacca americana)*

This weed grows in open woods, damp thickets, clearings and roadsides. Its berries and roots are poisonous, but if the shoots are gathered before turning pink, they can be boiled and eaten as greens. Sap from its berries were used as a dye and been used to color cheap wines.

Jack-in-the-Pulpit *(Arisaema triphyllum)*

Grows mainly in damp woods and swamps. Native Americans gathered the fleshy corms for food. This plant is peppery to the taste and causes a strong burning reaction if eaten raw, but this can be eliminated by cooking.

Poison Ivy *(Toxicodendron radicans)*

Normally found in wooded areas, it also grows in exposed rocky areas, open fields and disturbed areas. It is commonly eaten by many animals, and the seeds are consumed by birds. Contact dermatitis, the allergic reaction caused by poison ivy, can progress to anaphylaxis in extreme cases.

Eastern Poison Oak *(Toxicodendron pubescens)*

This native plant can be found growing in forests, thickets, and dry, sandy fields. Effects of poison oak contact are similar to those of poison ivy, beginning with severe itching, leading to inflammation, non-colored bumps, and then blistering. Its identifiable by its cluster of three leaves.

Flowering Trees

Eastern Redbud *(Cercis canadensis)*

Eastern Redbud is a native understory tree in mixed forests, producing bright pink, showy flowers in late Spring and early Summer. The flowers are pollinated by long-tongued bees such as blueberry and carpenter bees. Native Americans consumed redbud flowers raw or boiled, and ate roasted seeds.

Mountain Laurel *(Kalmia latifolia)*

A large, evergreen shrub, mountain laurel grows in open forests and rocky places. It is relatively tolerant of drought and can grow back vigorously after being stem-killed to the ground. It is long-lived; more than 100 annual rings have been reported in some examples.

Southern Catalpa *(Catalpa bignonioides)*

First cultivated in 1754, the wood was used for fence posts and railroad ties because of its resistance to rot and fast growth rate. The showy flowers are visited by hummingbirds and bees, and it is the sole host of the catalpa sphinx moth. It is easily recognized by its long, bean-like fruit.

Great Laurel *(Rhododendron maximum)*

This species, native to the Appalachians of the eastern U.S., affords protection to steep watersheds and shelter for wildlife with its densely tangled branches. The wood is very hard and is occasionally used for specialty wood products. The leaves can be poisonous, if ingested.

Flowering Dogwood *(Cornus florida)*

Dogwoods are native throughout temperate North America, particularly in the Southeast. The bark is rich in tannin and has been used as a substitute for quinine. Confederate soldiers would make a tea from the bark to treat pain and fevers, and used the leaves in a poultice to cover wounds.

Privet *(Ligustrum)*

There are almost 50 types of privet, often planted for hedges and landscape ornamentals. They are a non-native and highly invasive species, often displacing native vegetation. In large amounts, the odor from the flowers can cause respiratory irritation and allergic reactions.

Peach *(Prunus persica)*

This deciduous tree, native to northwest China, was brought to the Americas by Spanish explorers in the 16th century. However, they were not grown commercially until the early 19th century. Peach blossoms are high prized in Chinese culture, and play an integral role in folklore around the world.

Birds – Prey/Scavenger

Red-tailed Hawk *(Buteo jamaicensis)* Mature

Found in deciduous forests and open country, including farmlands. The most common of the hawks, it soars over open country searching for food, but will also hunt from a perch at the edge of open fields.

Cooper's Hawk *(Accipiter cooperii)*

Cooper's Hawks inhabit forests and woodland lots, but are comfortable in suburban areas with substantial tree cover. They hunt squirrels, chipmunks, and other rodents, but feed mainly on other birds. The males are responsible for the majority of nest-building, plus food for the female and their young.

Red-shouldered Hawk *(Buteo lineatus)*

Inhabits deciduous woodlands, especially where there is standing water. These raptors hunt from a low perch, dropping on their prey from above. They will return to the same nesting territory year after year.

American Kestrel *(Falco sparverius)*

Inhabit towns and cities, parks, farmlands and open country. This hawk prefers insects, small birds and rodents, capturing them on the ground rather than in midair like other falcons. Also known as the Sparrow Hawk.

Barred Owl *(Strix varia)*

Inhabits low, wet woodlands and swampy forests. Barred owls feed on rodents, birds, frogs and crayfish. A night hunter, it rests during the day, usually in a thick grove of trees. Generally sedentary, it will change locations if a Great Horned Owl moves into the area.

Turkey Vulture *(Cathartes aura)*

Found mainly in deciduous forests, woodlands and adjacent farmlands. Turkey Vultures use their keen sense of smell to locate carcasses. They are easy to distinguish from birds of prey by the "V" shape of their wings and unsteady wobble when in flight.

Black Vulture *(Coragyps atratus)*

Prefer open country, but breeds in light woodlands and thickets. Black vultures depend upon their eyesight to find food. Smaller, but more aggressive than turkey vultures in groups, they will often chase them away from a carcass. Black vultures are highly social birds with a strong sense of family.

Common Raven (*Corvus corax*)

Inhabits coniferous forests and rocky coasts. Ravens are primarily scavengers, and around towns may compete with gulls for garbage. However, they are very sensitive to human persecution and tend to avoid areas of heavy population.

American Crow *(Corvus brachyrhynchos)*

Found in woodlands, farmlands, suburban areas, and populated towns, the crow is intelligent, wary, and highly reproductive. They consume enormous amounts of grasshoppers, cutworms and other harmful insects. If caught young, crows can make interesting pets and some have learned to mimic the human voice.

Birds – Tree-Clinging

White-breasted Nuthatch *(Sitta carolinensis)*

They inhabit deciduous and mixed forests, feeding on seeds and small insects. The also enjoy congregating with chickadees and woodpeckers at the local feeder. Nuthatches feed upside down.

Downy Woodpecker *(Picoides pubescens)*

Preferring woodlands, parks and gardens, it is a familiar site amongst shade trees. It is the smallest and most abundant of the eastern woodpeckers. Due to their smaller size, they are able to eat foods that larger woodpeckers cannot reach.

Red-bellied Woodpecker *(Melanerpes carolinus)*

This bird inhabits open and swampy woodlands. Like most woodpeckers it is beneficial, eating large amounts of wood-boring beetles as well as other insect pests. It also feeds on acorns, beechnuts and wild fruits.

Yellow-bellied Sapsucker *(Sphyrapicus varius)*

Generally found in open deciduous forests, during migration, they may be found in parks and residential spaces. They gather sap by boring holes into the inner bark, letting the sap run out, and sucking or licking the sap with their tongues, along with any insects attracted to it.

Red-headed Woodpecker *(Melanerpes erythrocephalus)*

Prefers open country, farms, rural roads and open park-like woodlands. They often catch insects mid-air, and gather nuts and acorns, hiding them in holes and crevices. The Cherokee used this striking bird as a war symbol.

Northern Flicker *(Colaptes auratus)*

Flickers are members of the woodpecker family. You can look for the Northern Flicker in open habitats near trees, including woodlands, edges, yards, and parks. Because their main diet consists of ants and beetles, they are quite frequently found on the ground.

Birds – Perching

Gray Catbird *(Dumetella carolinensis)*

Heralding its presence with a cat-like whine, it can be found in thickets and brush, as well as residential areas and gardens. Catbirds are insectivorous, making them welcome in suburban areas. They will often respond to an imitation of their mewing call.

Northern Mockingbird *(Mimos polyglottos)*

Prefers residential areas, city parks, farmlands and open country with thickets. Gets its name from its ability to mimic the calls of various other birds. Mockingbirds are very territorial and, in addition to attacking various intruders, will often attack its own reflection.

Wood Thrush *(Hylocichla mustelina)*

A reclusive bird, the Wood Thrush lives in moist, deciduous woodlands with a thick underbrush and abundant leaf litter. It is an accomplished singer, and it has a y-shaped voicebox, allowing it to sing duets with itself. The male does most of the feeding, allowing the female to have a second brood.

Brown Thrasher *(Toxostoma rufum)*

Inhabits thickets, fields with scrub and woodland borders. Brown Thrashers may be confused with thrushes but are larger, have longer tails and are streaked, not spotted, below. They belong to the same family as the Mockingbird but are retiring and secretive.

American Robin *(Turdus migratorius)*

Can be found in towns, gardens, open woodlands and agricultural land, although they originally nested in forests. Robins generally breed twice a year, accounting for their large numbers. Although it is more noticeable in the Spring, this bird often winters in northern states.

Eastern Meadowlark *(Sturnella magna)*

Inhabits meadows and pastures, often nesting in hay fields. The meadowlark is polygamous so you may often find more than one female in the same nesting territory. Despite its name, this bird is not a lark; rather, it belongs to the blackbird family.

Red-winged Blackbird *(Agelaius phoeniceus)*

This bird generally prefers wetlands, both freshwater and saltwater, but can also be found in dry upland areas. The Red-winged Blackbird will aggressively defend its territory, often attacking much larger birds and humans. A pair will raise multiple broods per season, with a new nest each time.

European Starling *(Sturnus vulgaris)*

Inhabits cities, suburban areas and farmlands. Like the mockingbird, starlings can imitate the call of other birds. They are aggressive and will compete with native birds for food and habitat.

***Mourning Dove** (Zenaida macroura)*

Located in open fields, parks and lawns with many trees and shrubs. In some states it is hunted as a game bird, while in others it is protected as a songbird. Its species name, *macroura,* is Greek for "long-tailed."

Northern Cardinal *(Cardinalis cardinalis)*

Prefers thickets, brushy swampland, gardens and woodland edges. Seeds are their mainstay, but they will eat insects during the breeding season. Occupying their territory year-round, they are aggressive birds. Both sexes are accomplished songsters.

Blue Jay *(Cyanocitta cristata)*

Blue jays live chiefly in oak forests, but also occupy parks and suburban yards. They will bury seeds and acorns, regularly acting as tree planters when they neglect to retrieve their treasure. Their color comes not from pigment, but from the structure of their feathers and light interference.

Baltimore Oriole *(Icterus galbula)*

Look for this bird on the higher branches of deciduous trees in open woodland, orchards, and along the forest edge. Having adapted to humans, they often feed and nest in parks, orchards, and backyards, eating mostly fresh fruits and insects. The oriole builds an easily recognizable deep, sock-like hanging nest.

Eastern Towhee *(Pipilo erythrophthalmus)*

Towhees inhabit the underbrush in thickets, marshlands, and forest edges, where they scratch at the leaves to find their food, mainly seeds, fruits, and insects. They nest on the ground, and in tangled bushes such as honeysuckle and greenbrier; it's bright song may help with its location.

Common Yellowthroat *(Geothlypis trichas)*

Found in marshy areas, moist thickets, and low wetlands, they feast mainly on insects. They may be difficult to spot, but are curious enough to make an appearance if you make a low "phishing" sound. The yellowthroat has the distinction of being one of the first New World species catalogued.

Indigo Bunting *(Passerina cyanea)*

Indigo buntings prefer open brushy woodlands, old pastures, and forest edges near abandoned farmlands. Their color is attributed to light refraction and feather structure, rather than any blue pigment. This bird feeds on weed seeds, berries, and insect pests, making them beneficial to farmers and fruit growers.

Cedar Waxwing *(Bombycilla cedrorum)*

Cedar Waxwings can be found in woodlands, farms, orchards, and gardens where fruiting plants are located. Although they will eat insects, they can survive almost exclusively on fruit. They are social birds and will sometimes nest in clusters, with females doing most of the nest building.

Barn Swallow *(Hirundo rustica)*

Inhabits agricultural lands, marshes and lakeshores. They are swift and graceful fliers, catching insects in midair. Once building their nests in caves, barn swallows now build almost exclusively in man-made structures.

***Tufted Titmouse** (Baeolophus bicolor)*

Inhabits swampy or moist woodlands, but can be found near feeders during winter months. These birds are very social and usually join with small mixed flocks. Tufted titmice hoard food in the fall and winter. They take only one seed per trip and often shell them before storing.

Dark-eyed Junco *(Junco hyemalis)*

Easily recognized by its flashy white tail feathers, these small birds can be found in coniferous or mixed forests. Commonly called the snowbird, during the winter months, they are most visible in gardens, parks, and roadsides, foraging on the ground and beneath feeders.

Eastern Kingbird *(Tyrannus tyrannus)* Juvenile

Found in rangelands, forest edges and open grasslands. They often pursue flying insects and feed on berries. They are aggressive and will drive away birds larger than themselves including crows and hawks.

Black-capped Chickadee *(Poecile atricapillus)*

Lives in areas of deciduous and mixed forest, open woodlands and suburban areas, especially in winter. They enjoy the variety of food available in neighborhood feeders, but also feed on insect eggs and larvae, often clinging to branches upside down.

Olive-sided Flycatcher (*Contopus cooperi*)

Lives near boreal spruce and fir forests, usually near openings, ponds and bogs. This flycatcher almost always perches at or very near tops of the taller trees, in an exposed position on dead branches. Studies show that everything it eats is winged; it eats no caterpillars, spiders or larvae.

American Goldfinch *(Spinus tristis)*

Goldfinches prefer brushy thickets, weedy grasslands and nearby trees. The will also frequent suburban gardens, particularly when feeders containing sunflower and nyger seeds are present. Goldfinches are strict vegetarians, eating insects only by accident.

Eastern Bluebird *(Sialia sialis)*

Inhabits open woodlands and farmlands with scattered trees. They nest in tree cavities, old woodpecker holes, fence posts and bird boxes. Bluebirds will often have more than one brood in a season. Declining numbers have been offset recently by an effort to provide nesting boxes in many areas.

Ruby-throated Hummingbird *(Archilochus colubris)*

During the breeding season, this hummingbird can be found in deciduous and pine forests and forest edges, orchards, and gardens, where nectar is plentiful. They also eat small insects and spiders, a necessary source of protein. A hummingbird's wings can beat between 60 to 80 times per second.

Carolina Wren *(Thryothorus ludovicianus)*

The Carolina Wren frequents areas of tangled branches and leaves, garages and woodpiles, moving low to the ground. They feed on insects and spiders mostly, but will visit suet feeders. It is very vocal for such a shy bird, but it is only the males that sing. Wren pairs will mate for life.

Field Sparrow *(Spizella pusilla)*

Field Sparrows avoid nesting near humans, preferring to inhabit areas of tall grass and brush, abandoned fields, or thorny shrubs such as roses and briars. It can be distinguished from other sparrows by its pink bill and legs, and distinct white eye ring. It is found only in North America.

Song Sparrow *(Melospiza melodia)*

Inhabits thickets, pastures, garden undergrowth and city parks. The best known of the native sparrows, they are found almost everywhere. These birds are mainly monogamous and will search for a nest site as a pair.

House Sparrow *(Passer domesticus)*

First introduced in Central Park in the 1850s, the House Sparrow is one of the most common birds in North America. A menace to native species, they tend to congregate near houses, and are comfortable around humans. They eat most kinds of birdseed, especially millet, corn, and sunflower seed.

White-throated Sparrow *(Zonotrichia albicollis)*

Normally found in the brushy undergrowth near the forest edge, in winter it can readily be found in pastures and suburban areas. During the winter, they eat mainly seeds and fruits, often from backyard bird feeders, but during the summer they feast on large numbers of insects.

Birds – Water

Mallard *(Anas platyrhynchos)*

Generally located in ponds, lakes and marshes, they can be found on almost any body of water. Mallards frequently interbreed with domestic stock, producing a wide variety of patterns and colors. They eat water plants and small animals. Their life expectancy averages 20 years.

Canada Goose *(Branta canadensis)*

Inhabits wetlands and open grasslands, generally near lakes, bays, rivers and marshes. Canada geese mate for life and remain with their mate throughout the year. The young will remain with their parents for their entire first year.

Great Blue Heron *(Ardea herodias)*

The Great Blue, North America's largest heron, can be found in saltwater and freshwater habitats, including open coasts, marshes, and riverbanks.Although herons are monogamous within a single breeding season, they usually choose a new mate each year.

Killdeer (*Charadrius vociferus*)

Although considered a shorebird, Killdeer can often be found in open country with low vegetation, including plowed fields, golf courses and short-grass prairies. Adults will feign injury in order to lure predators away from their nest. The Killdeer derives its name from its distinctive call.

BIBLIOGRAPHY

Plant Sources:

Natural Resources Conservation Service PLANTS Database — http://plants.usda.gov

University of Texas at Austin Lady Bird Johnson Wildflower Center— Wildflower.org

Plants for a Future—PFAF.org

The Plants of Pennsylvania: An Illustrated Manual: Ann Fowler Rhoads, Timothy A. Block

National Audubon Society Field Guide to North American Wildflowers: John W. Thieret, William A. Niering, Nancy C. Olmstead

A Field Guide to Wildflowers: Northeastern and North-Central North America (Peterson Field Guides): Margaret McKenny and Roger Tory Peterson

USDA NRCS Plant Materials Program and John M. Row, Plant Materials Center, Manhattan, Kansas

Lee Allen Peterson, Edible Wild Plants, (New York City: Houghton Mifflin Company, 1977)

National Gardening Association —http://www.garden.org/plantguide

http://www.ceoe.udel.edu/nativeplantgarden/

http://www.americanmeadows.com

http://www.perennials.com

https://uswildflowers.com

http://www.mdflora.org

Plant Sources *(continued)***:**

EdibleWildFood.com

http://www.abnativeplants.com

http://www.bio.brandeis.edu/fieldbio

http://nativewildflowersandseeds.com

http://wildflowerinformation.org

Bird Sources:

Cornell University's Lab of Ornithology—allaboutbirds.org

National Geographic Field Guide to the Birds of North America: Jon Lloyd Dunn, Jonathan K. Alderfer

National Audubon Society Field Guide to North American Birds: Eastern Region, John Bull and John Farrrand, Jr.

http://www.audubon.org/field-guide/bird

http://animals.nationalgeographic.com/animals/birding/

www.whatbird.com

U.S. Fish and Wildlife Service— http://www.fws.gov

FLOWERS

BIRDS

While this book contains a large number of birds and flowers that can be found within the Gettysburg National Military Park, it does not contain them all. As I worked to compile photographs and identify each one, I discovered that there are several species that I have seen, but not yet photographed. Those will be saved for another day, and perhaps, another edition.